VEGAN COOKBOOK FOR ATHLETES

Breakfast – Lunch - Dinner

51 High-Protein Delicious Recipes for a Plant-Based Diet Plan and For a Strong Body While Maintaining Health, Vitality and Energy

VEGAN COOKBOOK FOR ATHLETES 1

51 HIGH-PROTEIN DELICIOUS RECIPES FOR A PLANT-BASED DIET PLAN AND FOR A STRONG BODY WHILE MAINTAINING HEALTH, VITALITY AND ENERGY 1

   DESCRIPTION 5
   INTRODUCTION TO THE VEGAN DIET 6
   BREAKFAST RECIPES 8
      Chocolate PB Smoothie 8
      Orange french toast 9
      Oatmeal Raisin Breakfast Cookie 12
      Berry Beetsicle Smoothie 14
      Blueberry Oat Muffins 15
      Quinoa Applesauce Muffins 18
      Pumpkin pancakes 20
      Green breakfast smoothie 22
      Blueberry Lemonade Smoothie 24
      Berry Protein Smoothie 25
      Blueberry and chia smoothie 27
      Green Kickstart Smoothie 28
      Warm Maple and Cinnamon Quinoa 30
      Warm Quinoa Breakfast Bowl 32
      Banana Bread Rice Pudding 34
      Apple and cinnamon oatmeal 36
      Mango Key Lime Pie Smoothie 37
      Spiced orange breakfast couscous 39
      Breakfast parfaits 41
      Sweet potato and
      Delicious Oat Mea
      Breakfast Cherry L
      Crazy Maple and F
      Hearty French Toa
      Tofu Burrito ....
      Tasty Mexican Bre
      Divine Carrot Oatmeal 59
      Wonderful Blueberry Butter 61
      Delicious Pumpkin Butter 63
   LUNCH RECIPES 65
      Amazing Potato Dish 67

Textured Sweet Potatoes and Lentils Delight 69
Incredibly Tasty Pizza 71
Rich Beans Soup 74
Delicious Baked Beans 76
Indian Lentils 78
Delicious Butternut Squash Soup 81
Amazing Mushroom Stew 83
Simple Tofu Dish 85
Special Jambalaya 87
Delicious Chard Soup 90
Chinese Tofu and Veggies 93
Wonderful Corn Chowder 96
Black Eyed Peas Stew 99
White Bean Cassoulet 102
Light Jackfruit Dish 105
Veggie Curry 107

DINNER RECIPES 110
Low Carb Peanut Dip (Instant Pot) 110
Spice-Rubbed Cauliflower (Instant Pot) 112
Satay Veggie Bowl 114
Shiritaki Noodles and Veggies 116
Shiritaki Alfredo 118
Taco-Spiced Stir-fry 120
Green-Glory Soup (Instant Pot) 122
Mediterranean-Style Pasta 124
Kale-Stuffed Mushroom Caps 126
Boiled Seasoned Veggies (Instant Pot) 128
Cauliflower Soup (Instant Pot) 130
Tahini Covered Eggplant 132

CONCLUSION 134

Description

As an athlete, it may sound like the vegan diet may not provide you the right Nutrition. But I am sure after reading these recipes; you can very well debunk that myth.

Inside this guide, there is a bunch of tasty and easy to cook recipes which will make sure that you get your share of protein and carbs. Remember that while being a meat free athlete ain't easy, this is hardly a reason to quit!

One of the greatest benefits of going vegan is the increased level of health you will experience and this manifests well beyond just your physique. Add to this the potent combination of healthy plant-based protein and you have a winner! You can also choose to supplement with vegan protein powder.

Remember to prep your meals ahead of time for maximum convenience. This guide covers the following recipes:
- Breakfast
- Lunch
- Dessert
- Desserts and snacks
- Sauces and dips

Happy Cooking!!

INTRODUCTION TO THE VEGAN DIET

A lot of people seeking to avoid a lifestyle that contributes to disorders and diseases such as heart attacks, type II diabetes and even cancer go Vegan. These people usually go vegan in order to reduce the intake of animal products and the harmful effects they can have on the body.

Most vegan products are plant based and they reduce the risk of these terrible diseases as well as lowering the risk of developing Alzheimer's disease and many others.

A Vegan diet also contributes to weight loss, not only is a plant-based diet less calorie dense, but provides the right nutrients to slim down quickly. A Vegan diet lowers cholesterol levels, LDLs and blood pressure - this will make you not only feel great, but look great too. In fact, people on a vegan diet typically have their blood pressure 25-75% lower than a person with an animal product diet. This also puts Vegans at a far lower risk of dementia.

Essentially, a Vegan diet will create a healthy lifestyle without even needing to work out. If you do work out as well though, that can produce some incredible results in terms of both weight loss and health! I will explore some of these benefits further later on in the book.

In addition, a lot of the antibiotics used in the modern animal farming system cause a lot of terrible side effects, and by going Vegan people are avoiding these.

For example, excess oestrogen, which is used in order to make animals more 'plump' to increase the meat industries 'yield', can contribute to weight gain when consumed by humans. In addition, high levels of oestrogen have been linked to gynecomastia (colloqually referred to as 'man boobs') in men.

BREAKFAST RECIPES

Chocolate PB Smoothie

Preparation time: 5 minutes
Cooking time: 0 minutes
Servings: 4
Ingredients
1 banana
¼ cup rolled oats, or 1 scoop plant protein powder
1 tablespoon flaxseed, or chia seeds
1 tablespoon unsweetened cocoa powder
1 tablespoon peanut butter, or almond or sunflower seed butter
1 tablespoon maple syrup (optional)
1 cup alfalfa sprouts, or spinach, chopped (optional)
½ cup non-dairy milk (optional)
1 cup water

Optional
1 teaspoon maca powder
1 teaspoon cocoa nibs

Directions

Purée everything in a blender until smooth, adding more water (or non-dairy milk) if needed. Add bonus boosters, as desired. Purée until blended.
Nutrition: calories: 474; protein: 13g; total fat: 16g; carbohydrates: 79g; fiber: 18g

Orange french toast

Preparation time: 15 minutes
Cooking time: 10 minutes
Servings: 4
Ingredients
3 very ripe bananas
1 cup unsweetened nondairy milk
Zest and juice of 1 orange
1 teaspoon ground cinnamon
¼ Teaspoon grated nutmeg
4 slices french bread
1 tablespoon coconut oil

Directions

In a blender, combine the bananas, almond milk, orange juice and zest, cinnamon, and nutmeg and blend until smooth. Pour the mixture into a 9-by-13-inch baking dish. Soak the bread in the mixture for 5 minutes on each side. While the bread soaks, heat a griddle or sauté pan over medium-high heat. Melt the coconut oil in the pan and swirl to coat. Cook the bread slices until golden brown on both sides, about 5 minutes each. Serve immediately.

Oatmeal Raisin Breakfast Cookie

Preparation time: 5 minutes
Cooking time: 15 minutes
Servings: 2 cookies
Ingredients
½ Cup rolled oats
1 tablespoon whole-grain flour
½ Teaspoon baking powder
1 to 2 tablespoons brown sugar
½ Teaspoon pumpkin pie spice or ground cinnamon (optional)
¼ Cup unsweetened applesauce, plus more as needed
2 tablespoons raisins, dried cranberries, or vegan chocolate chips

Directions

In a medium bowl, stir together the oats, flour, baking powder, sugar, and pumpkin pie spice (if using). Stir in the applesauce until thoroughly combined. Add another 1 to 2 tablespoons of applesauce if the mixture looks too dry (this will depend on the type of oats used).
Shape the mixture into 2 cookies. Put them on a microwave-safe plate and heat on high power for 90 seconds. Alternatively, bake on a small tray in a 350°f oven or toaster oven for 15 minutes. Let cool slightly before eating.
Nutrition (2 cookies): calories: 175; protein: 74g; total fat: 2g; saturated fat:0g; carbohydrates: 39g; fiber: 4g

Berry Beetsicle Smoothie

Preparation time: 3 minutes
Cooking time: 0minutes
Servings: 1
Ingredients
½ Cup peeled and diced beets
½ Cup frozen raspberries
1 frozen banana
1 tablespoon maple syrup
1 cup unsweetened soy or almond milk
Directions

Combine all the Ingredients in a blender and blend until smooth.

Blueberry Oat Muffins

Preparation time: 10 minutes
Cooking time: 20 minutes
Servings: 12 mufins

Ingredients
2 tablespoons coconut oil or vegan margarine, melted, plus more for preparing the muffin tin
1 cup quick-cooking oats or instant oats
1 cup boiling water
½ Cup nondairy milk
¼ Cup ground flaxseed
1 teaspoon vanilla extract
1 teaspoon apple cider vinegar
1½ cups whole-grain flour
½ Cup brown sugar
2 teaspoons baking soda
Pinch salt
1 cup blueberries

Directions

Preheat the oven to 400°f.
Coat a muffin tin with coconut oil, line with paper muffin cups, or use a nonstick tin.
In a large bowl, combine the oats and boiling water. Stir so the oats soften. Add the coconut oil, milk, flaxseed, vanilla, and vinegar and stir to combine. Add the flour, sugar, baking soda, and salt. Stir until just combined. Gently fold in the blueberries. Scoop the muffin mixture into the prepared tin, about ⅓ cup for each muffin.
Bake for 20 to 25 minutes, until slightly browned on top and springy to the touch. Let cool for about 10 minutes.
Run a dinner knife around the inside of each cup to loosen, then tilt the muffins on their sides in the muffin wells so air gets underneath. These keep in an airtight container in the refrigerator for up to 1 week or in the freezer indefinitely.

Nutrition (1muffin): calories: 174; protein: 5g; total fat: 3g; saturated fat:2g; carbohydrates: 33g; fiber: 4g

Quinoa Applesauce Muffins

Preparation time: 10 minutes
Cooking time: 15 minutes
Servings: 5
Ingredients
2 tablespoons coconut oil or margarine, melted, plus more for coating the muffin tin
¼ Cup ground flaxseed
½ Cup water
2 cups unsweetened applesauce
½ Cup brown sugar
1 teaspoon apple cider vinegar
2½ cups whole-grain flour
1½ cups cooked quinoa
2 teaspoons baking soda
Pinch salt
½ Cup dried cranberries or raisins
Directions

Preheat the oven to 400°f.
Coat a muffin tin with coconut oil, line with paper muffin cups, or use a nonstick tin. In a large bowl, stir together the flaxseed and water. Add the applesauce, sugar, coconut oil, and vinegar. Stir to combine. Add the flour, quinoa, baking soda, and salt, stirring until just combined. Gently fold in the cranberries without stirring too much. Scoop the muffin mixture into the prepared tin, about ⅓ cup for each muffin.

Bake for 15 to 20 minutes, until slightly browned on top and springy to the touch. Let cool for about 10 minutes. Run a dinner knife around the inside of each cup to loosen, then tilt the muffins on their sides in the muffin wells so air gets underneath. These keep in an airtight container in the refrigerator for up to 1 week or in the freezer indefinitely.
Per serving(1muffin): calories: 387; protein: 7g; total fat: 5g; saturated fat: 2g; carbohydrates: 57g; fiber: 8g

Pumpkin pancakes

Preparation time: 15 minutes
Cooking time: 15 minutes
Servings: 4
Ingredients
2 cups unsweetened almond milk
1 teaspoon apple cider vinegar
2½ cups whole-wheat flour
2 tablespoons baking powder
½ Teaspoon baking soda
1 teaspoon sea salt
1 teaspoon pumpkin pie spice or ½ teaspoon ground -cinnamon plus ¼ teaspoon grated -nutmeg plus ¼ teaspoon ground allspice
½ Cup canned pumpkin purée
1 cup water
1 tablespoon coconut oil

Directions

In a small bowl, combine the almond milk and apple cider vinegar. Set aside.
In a bowl, whisk together the flour, baking powder, baking soda, salt, and pumpkin pie spice. In bowl, combine the almond milk mixture, pumpkin purée, and water, whisking to mix well. Mix the wet Ingredients to the dry Ingredients and fold together until the dry -Ingredients are just moistened.
In a nonstick pan or griddle over medium-high heat, melt the coconut oil and swirl to coat. Pour the batter into the pan ¼ cup at a time and cook until the pancakes are browned, about 5 minutes per side. Serve immediately.

Green breakfast smoothie

Preparation time: 10 minutes
Cooking time: 0 minutes
Servings: 2
Ingredients
½ Banana, sliced
2 cups spinach or other greens, such as kale
1 cup sliced berries of your choosing, fresh or frozen
1 orange, peeled and cut into segments
1 cup unsweetened nondairy milk
1 cup ice

Directions
In a blender, combine all the Ingredients.
Starting with the blender on low speed, begin blending the smoothie, gradually increasing blender speed until smooth. Serve immediately.

Blueberry Lemonade Smoothie

Preparation time: 5 minutes
Cooking time: 0 minutes
Servings: 1

Ingredients
1 cup roughly chopped kale
¾ Cup frozen blueberries
1 cup unsweetened soy or almond milk
Juice of 1 lemon
1 tablespoon maple syrup
Directions

Combine all the Ingredients in a blender and blend until smooth. Enjoy immediately.

Berry Protein Smoothie

Preparation time: 5 minutes
Cooking time: 0 minutes
Servings: 1
Ingredients
1 banana
1 cup fresh or frozen berries
¾ Cup water or nondairy milk, plus more as needed
1 scoop plant-based protein powder, 3 ounces silken tofu, ¼ cup rolled oats, or ½ cup cooked quinoa

Additions
 1 tablespoon ground flaxseed or chia seeds
 1 handful fresh spinach or lettuce, or 1 chunk cucumber
Coconut water to replace some of the liquid

Directions:
In a blender, combine the banana, berries, water, and your choice of protein.
Add any addition Ingredients as desired. Purée until smooth and creamy, about 50 seconds.
Add a bit more water if you like a thinner smoothie.
Nutrition: calories: 332; protein: 7g; total fat: 5g; saturated fat: 1g; carbohydrates: 72g; fiber: 11g

Blueberry and chia smoothie

Preparation time: 10 minutes
Cooking time: 0 minutes
Servings: 2

Ingredients
2 tablespoons chia seeds
2 cups unsweetened nondairy milk
2 cups blueberries, fresh or frozen
2 tablespoons pure maple syrup or agave
2 tablespoons cocoa powder
Directions:
Soak the chia seeds in the almond milk for 5 minutes.
In a blender, combine the soaked chia seeds, almond milk, blueberries, maple syrup, and cocoa powder and blend until smooth. Serve immediately.

Green Kickstart Smoothie

Preparation time: 5 minutes
Cooking time: 0 minutes
Servings: 1
Ingredients
½ Avocado or 1 banana
½ Cup chopped cucumber, peeled if desired
1 handful fresh spinach or chopped lettuce
1 pear or apple, peeled and cored, or 1 cup unsweetened applesauce
2 tablespoons freshly squeezed lime juice
1 cup water or nondairy milk, plus more as needed
Additions
½-Inch piece peeled fresh ginger
1 tablespoon ground flaxseed or chia seeds
½ Cup soy yogurt or 3 ounces silken tofu
Coconut water to replace some of the liquid
2 tablespoons chopped fresh mint or ½ cup chopped mango
Directions:
In a blender, combine the avocado, cucumber, spinach, pear, lime juice, and water.
Add any Additions Ingredients as desired. Purée until smooth and creamy, about 50 seconds. Add a bit more water if you like a thinner smoothie.
Nutrition: calories: 263; protein: 4g; total fat: 14g; saturated fat: 2g; carbohydrates: 36g; fiber: 10g

Warm Maple and Cinnamon Quinoa

Preparation time: 5 minutes
Cooking time: 15 minutes
Servings: 4
Ingredients
1 cup unsweetened nondairy milk
1 cup water
1 cup quinoa, rinsed
1 teaspoon cinnamon
¼ Cup chopped pecans or other nuts or seeds, such as chia, sunflower seeds, or almonds
2 tablespoons pure maple syrup or agave
Directions:
In a medium saucepan over medium-high heat, bring the almond milk, water, and quinoa to a boil. Lower the heat to medium-low and cover. Simmer until the liquid is mostly absorbed and the quinoa softens, about 15 minutes.
Turn off the heat and allow to sit, covered, for 5 minutes. Stir in the cinnamon, pecans, and syrup. Serve hot.

Warm Quinoa Breakfast Bowl

Preparation time: 5 minutes
Cooking time: 0 minutes
Servings: 4
Ingredients
3 cups freshly cooked quinoa
1⅓ cups unsweetened soy or almond milk
2 bananas, sliced
1 cup raspberries
1 cup blueberries
½ Cup chopped raw walnuts
¼ Cup maple syrup
Directions:
Divide the Ingredients among 4 bowls, starting with a base of ¾ cup quinoa, ⅓ cup milk, ½ banana, ¼ cup raspberries, ¼ cup blueberries, and 2 tablespoons walnuts. Drizzle 1 tablespoon of maple syrup over the top of each bowl.

Banana Bread Rice Pudding

Preparation time: 5 minutes
Cooking time: 50 minutes
Servings: 4
Ingredients
1cup brown rice
1½ cups water
1½ cups nondairy milk
3 tablespoons sugar (omit if using a sweetened nondairy milk)
2 teaspoons pumpkin pie spice or ground cinnamon
2 bananas
3 tablespoons chopped walnuts or sunflower seeds (optional)
Directions

In a medium pot, combine the rice, water, milk, sugar, and pumpkin pie spice. Bring to a boil over high heat, turn the heat to low, and cover the pot. Simmer, stirring occasionally, until the rice is soft and the liquid is absorbed. White rice takes about 20 minutes; brown rice takes about 50 minutes.
Smash the bananas and stir them into the cooked rice. Serve topped with walnuts (if using). Leftovers will keep refrigerated in an airtight container for up to 5 days.
Nutrition: calories: 479; protein: 9g; total fat: 13g; saturated fat: 1g; carbohydrates: 86g; fiber: 7g

Apple and cinnamon oatmeal

Preparation time: 10 minutes
Cooking time: 10 minutes
Servings: 2
Ingredients
1¼ cups apple cider
1 apple, peeled, cored, and chopped
⅔ Cup rolled oats
1 teaspoon ground cinnamon
1 tablespoon pure maple syrup or agave (optional)
Directions

In a medium saucepan, bring the apple cider to a boil over medium-high heat. Stir in the apple, oats, and cinnamon. Bring the cereal to a boil and turn down heat to low. Simmer until the oatmeal thickens, 3 to 4 minutes. Spoon into two bowls and sweeten with maple syrup, if using. Serve hot.

Mango Key Lime Pie Smoothie

Preparation time: 5 minutes
Cooking time: 0 minutes
Servings: 1
Ingredients
¼ Avocado
1 cup baby spinach
½ Cup frozen mango chunks
1 cup unsweetened soy or almond milk
Juice of 1 lime (preferably a key lime).
1 tablespoon maple syrup
Directions

Combine all the **Ingredients** in a blender and blend until smooth. Enjoy immediately.

Spiced orange breakfast couscous

Preparation time: 10 minutes
Cooking time: 10 minutes
Servings: 4
Ingredients
3 cups orange juice
1½ cups couscous
1 teaspoon ground cinnamon
¼ Teaspoon ground cloves
½ Cup dried fruit, such as raisins or apricots
½ Cup chopped almonds or other nuts or seeds

Directions

In a small saucepan, bring the orange juice to a boil. Add the couscous, cinnamon, and cloves and remove from heat. Cover the pan with a lid and allow to sit until the -couscous softens, about 5 minutes.

Fluff the couscous with a fork and stir in the dried fruit and nuts. Serve -immediately.

Breakfast parfaits

Preparation time: 15 minutes
Cooking time: 0 minutes
Servings: 2
Ingredients
One 14-ounce can coconut milk, refrigerated overnight
1 cup granola
½ Cup walnuts
1 cup sliced strawberries or other seasonal berries
Directions
 Pour off the canned coconut-milk liquid and retain the solids.
 In two parfait glasses, layer the coconut-milk solids, granola, walnuts, and -strawberries. Serve immediately.

Sweet potato and kale hash

Preparation time: 10 minutes
Cooking time: 15 minutes
Servings: 2
Ingredients
1 sweet potato
2 tablespoons olive oil
½ Onion, chopped
1 carrot, peeled and chopped
2 garlic cloves, minced
½ Teaspoon dried thyme
1 cup chopped kale
Sea salt
Freshly ground black pepper
Directions

Prick the sweet potato with a fork and microwave on high until soft, about 5 minutes. Remove from the microwave and cut into ¼-inch cubes.
In a large nonstick sauté pan, heat the olive oil over medium-high heat. Add the onion and carrot and cook until softened, about 5 minutes. Add the garlic and thyme and cook until the garlic is fragrant, about 30 seconds.
Add the sweet potatoes and cook until the potatoes begin to brown, about 7 -minutes. Add the kale and cook just until it wilts, 1 to 2 minutes. Season with salt and pepper. Serve immediately.

Delicious Oat Meal

Preparation time: 10 minutes
Cooking time: 6 hours
Servings: 4
Ingredients:
3 cups water
3 cups almond milk
1 and ½ cups steel oats
4 dates, pitted and chopped
1 teaspoon cinnamon, ground
2 tablespoons coconut sugar
½ Teaspoon ginger powder
A pinch of nutmeg, ground
A pinch of cloves, ground
1 teaspoon vanilla extract
Directions:
Put water and milk in your slow cooker and stir.
Add oats, dates, cinnamon, sugar, ginger, nutmeg, cloves and vanilla extract, stir, cover and cook on low for 6 hours. Divide into bowls and serve for breakfast.
Enjoy!
Nutrition: calories 120, fat 1, fiber 2, carbs 3, protein 5

Breakfast Cherry Delight

Preparation time: 10 minutes
Cooking time: 8 hours and 10 minutes
Servings: 4
Ingredients:
2 cups almond milk
2 cups water
1 cup steel cut oats
2 tablespoons cocoa powder
1/3 cup cherries, pitted
¼ Cup maple syrup
½ Teaspoon almond extract

For the sauce:
2 tablespoons water
1 and ½ cups cherries, pitted and chopped
¼ Teaspoon almond extract

Directions:
Put the almond milk in your slow cooker.
Add 2 cups water, oats, cocoa powder, 1/3 cup cherries, maples syrup and ½ teaspoon almond extract.
Stir, cover and cook on low for 8 hours.
In a small pan, mix 2 tablespoons water with 1 and ½ cups cherries and ¼ teaspoon almond extract, stir well, bring to a simmer over medium heat and cook for 10 minutes until it thickens.
Divide oatmeal into breakfast bowls, top with the cherries sauce and serve.
Enjoy!
Nutrition: calories 150, fat 1, fiber 2, carbs 6, protein 5

Crazy Maple and Pear Breakfast

Preparation time: 10 minutes
Cooking time: 9 hours
Servings: 2
Ingredients:
1 pear, cored and chopped
½ Teaspoon maple extract
2 cups coconut milk
½ Cup steel cut oats
½ Teaspoon vanilla extract
1 tablespoon stevia
¼ Cup walnuts, chopped for serving
Cooking spray
Directions:
Spray your slow cooker with some cooking spray and add coconut milk.
Also, add maple extract, oats, pear, stevia and vanilla extract, stir, cover and cook on low for 9 hours.
Stir your oatmeal again, divide it into breakfast bowls and serve with chopped walnuts on top.
Enjoy!
Nutrition: calories 150, fat 3, fiber 2, carbs 6, protein 6

Hearty French Toast Bowls

Preparation time: 10 minutes
Cooking time: 5 hours
Servings: 4
Ingredients:
1 and ½ cups almond milk
1 cup coconut cream
1 tablespoon vanilla extract
½ Tablespoon cinnamon powder
2 tablespoons maple syrup
¼ Cup spenda
2 apples, cored and cubed
½ Cup cranberries, dried
1 pound vegan bread, cubed
Cooking spray

Directions:
Spray your slow cooker with some cooking spray and add the bread.
Also, add cranberries and apples and stir gently.
Add milk, coconut cream, maple syrup, vanilla extract, cinnamon powder and splenda.
Stir, cover and cook on low for 5 hours.
Divide into bowls and serve right away.
Enjoy!
Nutrition: calories 140, fat 2, fiber 3, carbs 6, protein 2

Tofu Burrito

Preparation time: 10 minutes
Cooking time: 8 hours
Servings: 4
Ingredients:
15 ounces canned black beans, drained
2 tablespoons onions, chopped
7 ounces tofu, drained and crumbled
2 tablespoons green bell pepper, chopped
½ Teaspoon turmeric
¾ Cup water
¼ Teaspoon smoked paprika
¼ Teaspoon cumin, ground
¼ Teaspoon chili powder
A pinch of salt and black pepper
4 gluten free whole wheat tortillas
Avocado, chopped for serving
Salsa for serving

Directions:
Put black beans in your slow cooker.
Add onions, tofu, bell pepper, turmeric, water, paprika, cumin, chili powder, a pinch of salt and pepper, stir, cover and cook on low for 8 hours.
Divide this on each tortilla, add avocado and salsa, wrap, arrange on plates and serve.
Enjoy!
Nutrition: calories 130, fat 4, fiber 2, carbs 5, protein 4

Tasty Mexican Breakfast

Preparation time: 10 minutes
Cooking time: 2 hours
Servings: 4
Ingredients:
1 cup brown rice
1 cup onion, chopped
2 cups veggie stock
1 red bell pepper, chopped
1 green bell pepper, chopped
4 ounces canned green chilies, chopped
15 ounces canned black beans, drained
A pinch of salt
Black pepper to the taste

For the salsa:
3 tablespoons lime juice
1 avocado, pitted, peeled and cubed
½ Cup cilantro, chopped
½ Cup green onions, chopped
½ Cup tomato, chopped
1 poblano pepper, chopped
2 tablespoons olive oil
½ Teaspoon cumin

Directions:
Put the stock in your slow cooker.
Add rice, onions and beans, stir, cover and cook on high for 1 hour and 30 minutes.
Add chilies, red and green bell peppers, a pinch of salt and black pepper, stir, cover again and cook on high for 30 minutes more.
Meanwhile, in a bowl, mix avocado with green onions, tomato, poblano pepper, cilantro, oil, cumin, a pinch of salt, black pepper and lime juice and stir really well.
Divide rice mix into bowls; top each with the salsa you've just made and serve.
Enjoy!
Nutrition: calories 140, fat 2, fiber 2, carbs 5, protein 5

Divine Carrot Oatmeal

Preparation time: 10 minutes
Cooking time: 7 hours
Servings: 3
Ingredients:
2 cups coconut milk
½ Cup old fashioned rolled oats
1 cup carrots, chopped
2 tablespoons agave nectar
1 teaspoon cardamom, ground
A pinch of saffron
Some chopped pistachios
Cooking spray
Directions:
Spray your slow cooker with some cooking spray and add coconut milk.
Also, add oats, carrots, agave nectar, cardamom and saffron.
Stir, cover and cook on Low for 7 hours.
Stir oatmeal again, divide into bowls and serve with chopped pistachios on top.
Enjoy!
Nutrition: calories 140, fat 2, fiber 2, carbs 4, protein 5

Wonderful Blueberry Butter

Preparation time: 10 minutes
Cooking time: 6 hours
Servings: 12
Ingredients:
5 cups blueberries puree
2 teaspoons cinnamon powder
Zest from 1 lemon
1 cup coconut sugar
½ Teaspoon nutmeg, ground
¼ Teaspoon ginger, ground

Directions:
Put blueberries in your slow cooker, cover and cook on low for 1 hour.
Stir your berries puree, cover and cook on low for 4 hours more.
Add sugar, ginger, nutmeg and lemon zest, stir and cook on high uncovered for 1 hour more.
Divide into jars, cover them and keep in a cold place until you serve it for breakfast.
Enjoy!
Nutrition: calories 143, fat 2, fiber 3, carbs 3, protein 4

Delicious Pumpkin Butter

Preparation time: 10 minutes
Cooking time: 4 hours
Servings: 5
Ingredients:
2 teaspoons cinnamon powder
4 cups pumpkin puree
1 and ¼ cup maple syrup
½ Teaspoon nutmeg
1 teaspoon vanilla extract

Directions:
In your slow cooker, mix pumpkin puree with maple syrup and vanilla extract, stir, cover and cook on high for 4 hours.
Add cinnamon and nutmeg, stir, divide into jars and serve for breakfast!
Enjoy!
Nutrition: calories 120, fat 2, fiber 2, carbs 4, protein 2

LUNCH RECIPES

Preparation time: 10 minutes
Cooking time: 3 hours
Servings: 4
Ingredients:
½ Cup quinoa
2 and ½ cups veggie stock
14 ounces canned tomatoes, chopped
15 ounces canned black beans, drained
¼ Cup green bell pepper, chopped
¼ Cup red bell pepper, chopped
A pinch of salt and black pepper
2 garlic cloves, minced
1 carrots, shredded
1 small chili pepper, chopped
2 teaspoons chili powder
1 teaspoon cumin, ground
A pinch of cayenne pepper
½ Cup corn
1 teaspoon oregano, dried

For the vegan sour cream:
A drizzle of apple cider vinegar
4 tablespoons water
½ Cup cashews, soaked overnight and drained
1 teaspoon lime juice

Directions:
Put the stock in your slow cooker.
Add quinoa, tomatoes, beans, red and green bell pepper, garlic, carrot, salt, pepper, corn, cumin, cayenne, chili powder, chili pepper and oregano, stir, cover and cook on High for 3 hours.
Meanwhile, put the cashews in your blender.
Add water, vinegar and lime juice and pulse really well.
Divide beans chili into bowls, top with vegan sour cream and serve.
Enjoy!
Nutrition: calories 300, fat 4, fiber 4, carbs 10, protein 7

Amazing Potato Dish

Preparation time: 10 minutes
Cooking time: 3 hours
Servings: 4
Ingredients:
1 and ½ pounds potatoes, peeled and roughly chopped
1 tablespoon olive oil
3 tablespoons water
1 small yellow onion, chopped
½ Cup veggie stock cube, crumbled
½ Teaspoon coriander, ground
½ Teaspoon cumin, ground
½ Teaspoon garam masala
½ Teaspoon chili powder
Black pepper to the taste
½ Pound spinach, roughly torn

Directions:
Put the potatoes in your slow cooker.
Add oil, water, onion, stock cube, coriander, cumin, garam masala, chili powder, black pepper and spinach.
Stir, cover and cook on High for 3 hours.
Divide into bowls and serve.
Enjoy!
Nutrition: calories 270, fat 4, fiber 6, carbs 8, protein 12

Textured Sweet Potatoes and Lentils Delight

Preparation time: 10 minutes
Cooking time: 4 hours and 30 minutes
Servings: 6
Ingredients:
6 cups sweet potatoes, peeled and cubed
2 teaspoons coriander, ground
2 teaspoons chili powder
1 yellow onion, chopped
3 cups veggie stock
4 garlic cloves, minced
A pinch of sea salt and black pepper
10 ounces canned coconut milk
1 cup water
1 and ½ cups red lentils
Directions:
Put sweet potatoes in your slow cooker.
Add coriander, chili powder, onion, stock, garlic, salt and pepper, stir, cover and cook on high for 3 hours.
Add lentils, stir, cover and cook for 1 hour and 30 minutes.
Add water and coconut milk, stir well, divide into bowls and serve right away.
Enjoy!
Nutrition: calories 300, fat 10, fiber 8, carbs 16, protein 10

Incredibly Tasty Pizza

Preparation time: 1 hour and 10 minutes
Cooking time: 1 hour and 45 minutes
Servings: 3
Ingredients:

For the dough:
½ Teaspoon italian seasoning
1 and ½ cups whole wheat flour
1 and ½ teaspoons instant yeast
1 tablespoon olive oil
A pinch of salt
½ Cup warm water
Cooking spray

For the sauce:
¼ Cup green olives, pitted and sliced
¼ Cup kalamata olives, pitted and sliced
½ Cup tomatoes, crushed
1 tablespoon parsley, chopped
1 tablespoon capers, rinsed
¼ Teaspoon garlic powder
¼ Teaspoon basil, dried
¼ Teaspoon oregano, dried
¼ Teaspoon palm sugar
¼ Teaspoon red pepper flakes
A pinch of salt and black pepper
½ Cup cashew mozzarella, shredded
Directions:

In your food processor, mix yeast with italian seasoning, a pinch of salt and flour.
Add oil and the water and blend well until you obtain a dough.
Transfer dough to a floured working surface, knead well, transfer to a greased bowl, cover and leave aside for 1 hour.
Meanwhile, in a bowl, mix green olives with kalamata olives, tomatoes, parsley, capers, garlic powder, oregano, sugar, salt, pepper and pepper flakes and stir well.
Transfer pizza dough to a working surface again and flatten it.
Shape so it will fit your slow cooker.
Grease your slow cooker with cooking spray and add dough.
Press well on the bottom.
Spread the sauce mix all over, cover and cook on high for 1 hour and 15 minutes.
Spread vegan mozzarella all over, cover again and cook on high for 30 minutes more.
Leave your pizza to cool down before slicing and serving it.
Nutrition: calories 340, fat 5, fiber 7, carbs 13, protein 15

Rich Beans Soup

Preparation time: 10 minutes
Cooking time: 7 hours
Servings: 4
Ingredients:
1 pound navy beans
1 yellow onion, chopped
4 garlic cloves, crushed
2 quarts veggie stock
A pinch of sea salt
Black pepper to the taste
2 potatoes, peeled and cubed
2 teaspoons dill, dried
1 cup sun-dried tomatoes, chopped
1 pound carrots, sliced
4 tablespoons parsley, minced
Directions:
Put the stock in your slow cooker.
Add beans, onion, garlic, potatoes, tomatoes, carrots, dill, salt and pepper, stir, cover and cook on low for 7 hours.
Stir your soup, add parsley, divide into bowls and serve.
Enjoy!
Nutrition: calories 250, fat 4, fiber 3, carbs 9, protein 10

Delicious Baked Beans

Preparation time: 10 minutes
Cooking time: 12 hours
Servings: 8
Ingredients:
1 pound navy beans, soaked overnight and drained
1 cup maple syrup
1 cup bourbon
1 cup vegan bbq sauce
1 cup palm sugar
¼ Cup ketchup
1 cup water
¼ Cup mustard
¼ Cup blackstrap molasses
¼ Cup apple cider vinegar
¼ Cup olive oil
2 tablespoons coconut aminos
Directions:
Put the beans in your slow cooker.
Add maple syrup, bourbon, bbq sauce, sugar, ketchup, water, mustard, molasses, vinegar, oil and coconut aminos. Stir everything, cover and cook on Low for 12 hours.
Divide into bowls and serve.
Enjoy!
Nutrition: calories 430, fat 7, fiber 8, carbs 15, protein 19

Indian Lentils

Preparation time: 10 minutes
Cooking time: 3 hours
Servings: 4
Ingredients:
1 yellow bell pepper, chopped
1 sweet potato, chopped
2 and ½ cups lentils, already cooked
4 garlic cloves, minced
1 yellow onion, chopped
2 teaspoons cumin, ground
15 ounces canned tomato sauce
½ Teaspoon ginger, ground
A pinch of cayenne pepper
1 tablespoons coriander, ground
1 teaspoon turmeric, ground
2 teaspoons paprika
2/3 cup veggie stock
1 teaspoon garam masala
A pinch of sea salt
Black pepper to the taste
Juice of 1 lemon

Directions:
Put the stock in your slow cooker.
Add potato, lentils, onion, garlic, cumin, bell pepper, tomato sauce, salt, pepper, ginger, coriander, turmeric, paprika, cayenne, garam masala and lemon juice.
Stir, cover and cook on high for 3 hours.
Stir your lentils mix again, divide into bowls and serve.
Enjoy!
Nutrition: calories 300, fat 6, fiber 5, carbs 9, protein 12

Delicious Butternut Squash Soup

Preparation time: 10 minutes
Cooking time: 6 hours
Servings: 8
Ingredients:
1 apple, cored, peeled and chopped
½ Pound carrots, chopped
1 pound butternut squash, peeled and cubed
1 yellow onion, chopped
A pinch of sea salt
Black pepper to the taste
1 bay leaf
3 cups veggie stock
14 ounces canned coconut milk
¼ Teaspoon sage, dried
Directions:
Put the stock in your slow cooker.
Add apple squash, carrots, onion, salt, pepper and bay leaf.
Stir, cover and cook on low for 6 hours.
Transfer to your blender, add coconut milk and sage and pulse really well.
Ladle into bowls and serve right away.
Enjoy!
Nutrition: calories 200, fat 3, fiber 6, carbs 8, protein 10

Amazing Mushroom Stew

Preparation time: 10 minutes
Cooking time: 8 hours
Servings: 4
Ingredients:
2 garlic cloves, minced
1 celery stalk, chopped
1 yellow onion, chopped
1 and ½ cups firm tofu, pressed and cubed
1 cup water
10 ounces mushrooms, chopped
1 pound mixed peas, corn and carrots
2 and ½ cups veggie stock
1 teaspoon thyme, dried
2 tablespoons coconut flour
A pinch of sea salt
Black pepper to the taste
Directions:
Put the water and stock in your slow cooker.
Add garlic, onion, celery, mushrooms, mixed veggies, tofu, thyme, salt, pepper and flour.
Stir everything, cover and cook on low for 8 hours.
Divide into bowls and serve hot.
Enjoy!
Nutrition: calories 230, fat 4, fiber 6, carbs 10, protein 7

Simple Tofu Dish

Preparation time: 10 minutes
Cooking time: 3 hours
Servings: 6
Ingredients:
1 big tofu package, cubed
1 tablespoon sesame oil
¼ Cup pineapple, cubed
1 tablespoon olive oil
2 garlic cloves, minced
1 tablespoons brown rice vinegar
2 teaspoon ginger, grated
¼ Cup soy sauce
5 big zucchinis, cubed
¼ Cup sesame seeds
Directions:
In your food processor, mix sesame oil with pineapple, olive oil, garlic, ginger, soy sauce and vinegar and whisk well.
Add this to your slow cooker and mix with tofu cubes.
Cover and cook on High for 2 hours and 45 minutes.
Add sesame seeds and zucchinis, stir gently, cover and cook on High for 15 minutes.
Divide between plates and serve.
Enjoy!
Nutrition: calories 200, fat 3, fiber 4, carbs 9, protein 10

Special Jambalaya

Preparation time: 10 minutes
Cooking time: 6 hours
Servings: 4
Ingredients:
6 ounces soy chorizo, chopped
1 and ½ cups celery ribs, chopped
1 cup okra
1 green bell pepper, chopped
16 ounces canned tomatoes and green chilies, chopped
2 garlic cloves, minced
½ Teaspoon paprika
1 and ½ cups veggie stock
A pinch of cayenne pepper
Black pepper to the taste
A pinch of salt
3 cups already cooked wild rice for serving

Directions:
Heat up a pan over medium high heat, add soy chorizo, stir, brown for a few minutes and transfer to your slow cooker.
Also, add celery, bell pepper, okra, tomatoes and chilies, garlic, paprika, salt, pepper and cayenne to your slow cooker.
Stir everything, add veggie stock, cover the slow cooker and cook on low for 6 hours.
Divide rice on plates, top each serving with your vegan jambalaya and serve hot.
Enjoy!
Nutrition: calories 150, fat 3, fiber 7, carbs 15, protein 9

Delicious Chard Soup

Preparation time: 10 minutes
Cooking time: 8 hours
Servings: 6
Ingredients:
1 yellow onion, chopped
1 tablespoon olive oil
1 celery stalk, chopped
2 garlic cloves, minced
1 carrot, chopped
1 bunch swiss chard, torn
1 cup brown lentils, dried
5 potatoes, peeled and cubed
1 tablespoon soy sauce
Black pepper to the taste
A pinch of sea salt
6 cups veggie stock

Directions:
Heat up a big pan with the oil over medium high heat, add onion, celery, garlic, carrot and Swiss chard, stir, cook for a few minutes and transfer to your slow cooker.
Also, add lentils, potatoes, soy sauce, salt, pepper and stock to the slow cooker, stir, cover and cook on Low for 8 hours.
Divide into bowls and serve hot.
Enjoy!
Nutrition: calories 200, fat 4, fiber 5, carbs 9, protein 12

Chinese Tofu and Veggies

Preparation time: 10 minutes
Cooking time: 4 hours
Servings: 4
Ingredients:
14 ounces extra firm tofu, pressed and cut into medium triangles
Cooking spray
2 teaspoons ginger, grated
1 yellow onion, chopped
3 garlic cloves, minced
8 ounces tomato sauce
¼ Cup hoisin sauce
¼ Teaspoon coconut aminos
2 tablespoons rice wine vinegar
1 tablespoon soy sauce
1 tablespoon spicy mustard
¼ Teaspoon red pepper, crushed
2 teaspoons molasses
2 tablespoons water
A pinch of black pepper
3 broccoli stalks
1 green bell pepper, cut into squares
2 zucchinis, cubed

Directions:
Heat up a pan over medium high heat, add tofu pieces, brown them for a few minutes and transfer to your slow cooker.
Heat up the pan again over medium high heat, add ginger, onion, garlic and tomato sauce, stir, sauté for a few minutes and transfer to your slow cooker as well.
Add hoisin sauce, aminos, vinegar, soy sauce, mustard, red pepper, molasses, water and black pepper, stir gently, cover and cook on high for 3 hours.
Add zucchinis, bell pepper and broccoli, cover and cook on high for 1 more hour.
Divide between plates and serve right away.

Enjoy!
Nutrition: calories 300, fat 4, fiber 8, carbs 14, protein 13

Wonderful Corn Chowder

Preparation time: 10 minutes
Cooking time: 8 hours and 30 minutes
Servings: 6
Ingredients:
2 cups yellow onion, chopped
2 tablespoons olive oil
1 red bell pepper, chopped
1 pound gold potatoes, cubed
1 teaspoon cumin, ground
4 cups corn kernels
4 cups veggie stock
1 cup almond milk
A pinch of salt
A pinch of cayenne pepper
½ Teaspoon smoked paprika
Chopped scallions for serving

Directions:
Heat up a pan with the oil over medium heat, add onion, stir and sauté for 5 minutes and then transfer to your slow cooker.
Add bell pepper, 1 cup corn, potatoes, paprika, cumin, salt and cayenne, stir, cover and cook on low for 8 hours.
Blend this using an immersion blender and then mix with almond milk and the rest of the corn.
Stir chowder, cover and cook on low for 30 minutes more.
Ladle into bowls and serve with chopped scallions on top.

Enjoy!
Nutrition: calories 200, fat 4, fiber 7, carbs 13, protein 16

Black Eyed Peas Stew

Preparation time: 10 minutes
Cooking time: 4 hours
Servings: 8
Ingredients:
3 celery stalks, chopped
2 carrots, sliced
1 yellow onion, chopped
1 sweet potato, cubed
1 green bell pepper, chopped
3 cups black-eyed peas, soaked for 8 hours and drained
1 cup tomato puree
4 cups veggie stock
A pinch of salt
Black pepper to the taste
1 chipotle chile, minced
1 teaspoon ancho chili powder
1 teaspoons sage, dried and crumbled
2 teaspoons cumin, ground
Chopped coriander for serving

Directions:
Put celery in your slow cooker.
Add carrots, onion, potato, bell pepper, black-eyed peas, tomato puree, salt, pepper, chili powder, sage, chili, cumin and stock.
Stir, cover and cook on High for 4 hours.
Stir stew again, divide into bowls and serve with chopped coriander on top.
Enjoy!
Nutrition: calories 200, fat 4, fiber 7, carbs 9, protein 16

White Bean Cassoulet

Preparation time: 10 minutes
Cooking time: 6 hours
Servings: 4
Ingredients:
2 celery stalks, chopped
3 leeks, sliced
4 garlic cloves, minced
2 carrots, chopped
2 cups veggie stock
15 ounces canned tomatoes, chopped
1 bay leaf
1 tablespoon italian seasoning
30 ounces canned white beans, drained

For the breadcrumbs:
Zest from 1 lemon, grated
1 garlic clove, minced
2 tablespoons olive oil
1 cup vegan bread crumbs
¼ Cup parsley, chopped

Directions:

Heat up a pan with a splash of the veggie stock over medium heat, add celery and leeks, stir and cook for 2 minutes.
Add carrots and garlic, stir and cook for 1 minute more.
Add this to your slow cooker and mix with stock, tomatoes, bay leaf, italian seasoning and beans.
Stir, cover and cook on low for 6 hours.
Meanwhile, heat up a pan with the oil over medium high heat, add bread crumbs, lemon zest, 1 garlic clove and parsley, stir and toast for a couple of minutes.
Divide your white beans mix into bowls, sprinkle bread crumbs mix on top and serve.
Enjoy!
Nutrition: calories 223, fat 3, fiber 7, carbs 10, protein 7

Light Jackfruit Dish

Preparation time: 10 minutes
Cooking time: 6 hours
Servings: 4
Ingredients:
40 ounces green jackfruit in brine, drained
½ Cup agave nectar
½ Cup gluten free tamari sauce
¼ Cup soy sauce
1 cup white wine
2 tablespoons ginger, grated
8 garlic cloves, minced
1 pear, cored and chopped
1 yellow onion, chopped
½ Cup water
4 tablespoons sesame oil
Directions:
Put jackfruit in your slow cooker.
Add agave nectar, tamari sauce, soy sauce, wine, ginger, garlic, pear, onion, water and oil.
Stir well, cover and cook on low for 6 hours.
Divide jackfruit mix into bowls and serve.
Enjoy!
Nutrition: calories 160, fat 4, fiber 1, carbs 10, protein 3

Veggie Curry

Preparation time: 10 minutes
Cooking time: 4 hours
Servings: 4

Ingredients:
1 tablespoon ginger, grated
14 ounces canned coconut milk
Cooking spray
16 ounces firm tofu, pressed and cubed
1 cup veggie stock
¼ Cup green curry paste
½ Teaspoon turmeric
1 tablespoon coconut sugar
1 yellow onion, chopped
1 and ½ cup red bell pepper, chopped
A pinch of salt
¾ Cup peas
1 eggplant, chopped

Directions:
Put the coconut milk in your slow cooker.
Add ginger, stock, curry paste, turmeric, sugar, onion, bell pepper, salt, peas and eggplant pieces, stir, cover and cook on high for 4 hours.
Meanwhile, spray a pan with cooking spray and heat up over medium high heat.
Add tofu pieces and brown them for a few minutes on each side.
Divide tofu into bowls, add slowly cooked curry mix on top and serve.
Enjoy!
Nutrition: calories 200, fat 4, fiber 6, carbs 10, protein 9

DINNER RECIPES

Low Carb Peanut Dip (Instant Pot)

Servings: 6
Preparation time: 10 minutes
Nutrition
Calories: 451 kcal
Carbs: 18.9g
Fat: 37.7g
Protein: 9.8g
Fiber: 4.9g
Sugar: 3.7g
Ingredients:
2 tbsp. Peanut oil
1 cup peanut cheese spread
1 low carb crust
1 cup onion (chopped)
1 tbsp. Garlic (minced)
1 cup fire roasted tomatoes
1 tbsp. Chipotle pepper (chopped)
½ Cup water
1 tbsp. Chili powder
2 tsp. Ground cumin
2 tsp. Salt
1 tsp. Dried oregano
Total number of **Ingredients**: 12

Directions:

Select the "sauté" option on the instant pot, waiting till it reads "hot" to add the onions and garlic with olive oil, stirring for about 30 minutes.

Blend the canned tomatoes and the peanut butter until it is relatively smooth.

Mix the cumin, salt, chili powder, and oregano; then mix with the onions and garlic for 30 seconds, allowing them to soak in the flavor.

Pour the blender mix into the pot along with the water.

Close the pot and cook on instant pressure for 10 minutes, allowing natural pressure release for 10 minutes after that.

Mix well, and serve with a low carb crust for dipping!

Spice-Rubbed Cauliflower (Instant Pot)

Servings: 4
Preparation time: 10 minutes
Nutrition
Calories: 86 kcal
Carbs: 12.3g
Fat: 2.7g
Protein: 3.3g
Fiber: 7.5g
Sugar: 5.6g

Ingredients:
2 lbs. Cauliflower
2 tbsp. Olive oil
2 tsp. Paprika
2 tsp. Ground cumin
Salt to taste
1 cup cilantro (fresh, chopped)
1 lemon (quartered)
Total number of **Ingredients**: 7

Directions:
Insert the steam rack in the instant pot, adding 1 ½ cups of water.

Remove the leaves of the cauliflower, cut the end from the base, and place on the steam rack.
Combine the oil, salt, paprika, and cumin in a bowl; then pour over the cauliflower to coat.
Lock the lid and cook under pressure for 4 minutes; use the quick release to let out the steam, and open the lid. Take the cauliflower out and cut it into 1 inch sized "steaks."
Divide onto plates, sprinkle the cilantro on top, and place a quartered lemon on each plate.

Satay Veggie Bowl

Servings: 4
Preparation time: 15 minutes
Nutrition
Calories: 605 kcal
Carbs: 16g
Fat: 53.1g
Protein: 15.9g
Fiber: 9.8g
Sugar: 4.7g
Ingredients:
Handful of olives
Olive oil, garlic powder, and salt to taste
1 cup broccoli (florets)
1 cup spinach (frozen)
3 cups peanut butter or cashew cheese
Total number of **Ingredients:** 5
Directions:
In a greased skillet, add broccoli, and frozen spinach. Adding salt and garlic powder to taste, mix well and wait until the spinach has softened and the tempeh is cooked. Transfer to a bowl, and add olive oil, garlic powder, and salt to taste. Garnish with olives.

Shiritaki Noodles and Veggies

Servings: 1
Preparation time: 15 minutes
Nutrition
Calories: 279 kcal
Carbs: 13.5g
Fat: 28.2g
Protein: 3.0g
Fiber: 4.6g
Sugar: 5.2g
Ingredients:
1 package shiritaki noodles (rinsed, drained)
2 tbsp. Peanut oil
¼ Cup marinara sauce
½ Cup mixed veggies (of choice)
Total number of **Ingredients:** 4
Directions:
Boil the noodles until soft.
Once done, transfer to a skillet and add the marinara sauce, oil, and mixed veggies.
Keep mixing, letting the mixture heat until the veggies are warm and incorporated.

Shiritaki Alfredo

Servings: 1
Preparation time: 10 minutes
Nutrition
Calories: 377 kcal
Carbs: 11.3g
Fat: 34.3g
Protein: 5.6g
Fiber: 5.5g
Sugar: 1.0g
Ingredients:
1 package shiritaki noodles (rinsed, drained)
2 tbsp. Olive oil
¼ Cup vegan cream cheese
1 cup spinach (frozen)
Salt, pepper, and garlic powder (to taste)
Almond milk (to reach desired consistency)
Total number of **Ingredients:** 8
Directions:
Dump all Ingredients in a pan with olive oil and slowly add almond milk for a creamy feel.
Once all Ingredients are mixed and the milk thickens, turn off the heat and serve.

Taco-Spiced Stir-fry

Servings: 1
Preparation time: 15 minutes
Nutrition
Calories: 293 kcal
Carbs: 18.7g
Fat: 22.5g
Protein: 4.0g
Fiber: 10.5g
Sugar: 3.7g
Ingredients:
1 package cauliflower rice
1 tbsp. Peanut oil
1 tbsp. Taco seasoning
½ Tbsp. Chili powder
2 tbsp. Guacamole
¼ Cup sliced olives
Total number of **Ingredients:** 6
Directions:
Mix all Ingredients, except the guacamole and olives, in a pan on medium heat until the cauliflower rice has softened. Take off the stove and it cool when rice has softened, before serving.

Green-Glory Soup (Instant Pot)

Servings: 6
Preparation time: 15 minutes
Nutrition
Calories: 284 kcal
Carbs: 9.1g
Fat: 26.3g
Protein: 2.9g
Fiber: 3.1g
Sugar: 5.3g
Ingredients:
1 head cauliflower (florets)
1 onion (diced)
2 cloves garlic (minced)
1 cup spinach (fresh or frozen)
1 bay leaf (crumbled)
1 cup coconut milk
4 cups vegetable stock
Salt and pepper to taste
Herbs for garnish (optional)
½ Cup coconut oil
Total number of **Ingredients:** 11

Directions:

In a pressure pot on "sauté" mode, sauté onions and garlic until onions are browned. Once cooked, add the cauliflower and bay leaf and cook for about 5 minutes, stirring occasionally.

Add the spinach and continue cooking and stirring for 5 minutes.

Pour in the vegetable stock and set the timer for 10 minutes on high pressure to let the mix come to a boil; then allow quick pressure release and add the coconut milk.

Season with garnishes of choice as well as salt and pepper. Turn off the pot and mix the soup until it becomes thick and creamy with a hand blender.

Mediterranean-Style Pasta

Servings: 4
Preparation time: 10 minutes
Nutrition
Calories: 117 kcal
Carbs: 7.9g
Fat: 8.7g
Protein: 1.8g
Fiber: 2.6g
Sugar: 4.2g

Ingredients:
2 zucchinis (large, spiral-sliced)
1 cup spinach
2 tbsp. Olive oil
5 cloves garlic (minced)
Salt and pepper (to taste)
¼ Cup tomatoes (sun dried for added flavor)
2 tbsp. Capers
2 tbsp. Parsley (chopped)
10 kalamata olives (halved)
Total number of **Ingredients:** 10

Directions:
In a lightly oiled pan, add the spinach, zucchini, salt, pepper, and garlic, sautéing until the zucchini is tender; drain the excess liquid.
Add tomatoes, capers, olives, and parsley, mixing for about 3 minutes.
Remove from heat and toss well before serving, adding more or less of any item for preference.

Kale-Stuffed Mushroom Caps

Servings: 2
Preparation time: 15 minutes
Nutrition
Calories: 81 kcal
Carbs: 7.3g
Fat: 4.8g
Protein: 3g
Fiber: 2.2g
Sugar: 1.1g

Ingredients:
4 cups kale (fresh, chopped)
2 tbsp. Olive oil
3 tsp. Garlic (minced)
1 tsp. Garlic powder
½ Tsp. Salt
4 portobello mushroom caps (large)
Total number of **Ingredients:** 6

Directions:
Sauté the garlic and olive oil in a pan. Before it burns, add the kale, stirring well for about 7 minutes. Then add the garlic powder and salt, stirring well for 3 more minutes. Turn off the heat.
Mix the other half of the olive oil and garlic, then rub on the mushroom caps.
Place caps on the grill on medium heat, allowing them to cook for about 10 minutes—5 minutes per side—until tender.
Remove from the grill and divide your kale mixture on top of each cap; serve and enjoy.

Check out this recipe for a delicious, unique treat to spice up any dinner or gathering.

Boiled Seasoned Veggies (Instant Pot)

Servings: 1
Preparation time: 15 minutes
Nutrition
Calories: 816 kcal
Carbs: 66.1g
Fat: 55.8g
Protein: 12.5g
Fiber: 26.9g
Sugar: 32.2g

Ingredients:
1 eggplant (cubed, medium)
2 zucchinis (halved and sliced)
8 oz. Mushrooms (of choice, quartered)
6 cloves garlic (minced)
3 sprigs fresh rosemary (chopped)
¼ Cup olive oil
2 tbsp. Balsamic vinegar
2 tbsp. Dried onion flakes
½ Cup water
Salt and pepper to taste
Total number of **Ingredients:** 11

Directions:

Preheat oven to 400°f.

In a bowl, mix all Ingredients, lightly tossing and making sure all the vegetables are coated in spices and olive oil.

Throw mixture in a pressure pot with ½ cup of water and cook on high pressure for about 20 minutes, allowing for natural pressure release once time is up.

Open, and add more or less of the spices you prefer.

If you're a veggie lover, you are sure to love this dish. Vegetables are heart-healthy, filling, and kind alternatives to other non-vegan or ketogenic meals!

Cauliflower Soup (Instant Pot)

Servings: 6
Preparation time: 10 minutes
Nutrition
Calories: 43 kcal
Carbs: 4.3g
Fat: 2.2g
Protein: 1.4g
Fiber: 1.3g
Sugar: 2.2g
Ingredients:
3 cups vegetable stock
2 tsp. Thyme powder
½ Tsp. Matcha green tea powder
1 head cauliflower (about 2.5 cups, florets)
1 tbsp. Olive oil
5 garlic cloves (minced)
Salt and pepper to taste
Total number of **Ingredients:** 8

Directions:
In an instant pressure pot, add the vegetable stock, thyme, and matcha powder on medium heat. Bring to a boil.
Add the cauliflower and set timer for 10 minutes on high pressure, allowing for quick pressure release when finished. In a saucepan, add garlic and olive oil until tender, and you can smell it; then add it to the pot along with salt and cook for 1 to 2 minutes.
Turn off the heat and. Blend the soup until smooth and creamy with a blender.

Tahini Covered Eggplant

Servings: 1
Preparation time: 20 minutes
Nutrition
Calories: 474 kcal
Carbs: 41.9g
Fat: 31.2g
Protein: 6.3g
Fiber: 21.9g
Sugar: 17.9g

Ingredients:
1 eggplant (sliced)
1 garlic clove (minced)
1 tbsp. Olive oil
Salt and pepper (to taste)
½ Cup chopped parsley
Sauce:
1 tsp. Olive oil
1 onion (chopped)
½ Garlic clove (chopped)
Handful of parsley (chopped)
⅓ Cup almond milk
1 tsp. Tahini
Salt (to taste)
Total number of **Ingredients:** 12

Directions:

Preheat oven to 350°f.

Mix all Ingredients in a medium bowl with the eggplant.

Place on baking tray, and bake for 30 minutes.

Sauce:

Blend all Ingredients. Add more or less to taste.

CONCLUSION

There you have it. You are now well on your way to weight the Vegan way!

Be prepared to feel great, have energy you never had before and achieve the weight loss results you always desired! Thank you for taking the time to read my book and stay tuned for more books on Veganism in the future.

Thanks again for your support!

www.ingramcontent.com/pod-product-compliance
Lightning Source LLC
Chambersburg PA
CBHW070916080526
44589CB00013B/1313